W9-CNP-165

A Children's Book About

GOSSIPING

Managing Editor: Ellen Klarberg
Copy Editor: Annette Gooch
Editorial Assistant: Lana Eberhard
Art Director: Jennifer Wiezel
Production Artist: Gail Miller
Illustration Designer: Bartholomew
Inking Artist: Micah Schwaberow
Coloring Artist: Christine McNamara
Lettering Artist: Linda Hanney
Typographer: Communication Graphics

Copyright ©1988 Joy Berry

No part of this book may be reproduced by any mechanical,
photographic or electronic process, or in the form of a
phonographic recording, nor may it be stored in a retrieval system,
transmitted, or otherwise be copied for public or private use
without the written permission of the publisher.

Printed in 1991

A Children's Book About

GOSSIPING

By Joy Berry

GROLIER ENTERPRISES CORP.

This book is about Katie and her friends Laura and Tommy.

Reading about Katie and her friends can help you understand and deal with **gossiping.**

You are gossiping when you tell others
unkind things about someone.

You are gossiping when you tell others untrue things about someone.

Gossiping can hurt the people you gossip about.

The things you say may cause them to feel bad about themselves.

MAYBE LAURA IS RIGHT. MAYBE I AM A CRYBABY. I FEEL AWFUL.
YOU DON'T LOOK SO GOOD.

The people you gossip about can be hurt in another way.

The things you say may cause others to treat them unkindly.

DO YOU WANT TO PLAY?
NO, THANKS.
YOU'RE JUST A CRYBABY!
I HOPE HE DOESN'T THINK I'M A SCAREDY-CAT.

Gossiping can hurt you. If you say unkind things, people might think you are unkind. They might not like you. They might not want to be with you.

Gossiping can hurt you in another way. Others might think you are dishonest if what you say is not true. They might not trust you. They might not believe anything you say.

Gossiping can hurt others and it can hurt you. Do not gossip. Here is a good rule for you to follow:

If you cannot say something nice, do not say anything at all.

Some people may ask you questions about other people so that you will gossip. Do not gossip when this happens. Do these things instead:

- Explain kindly that you would rather not answer questions about others.
- Then suggest that you talk about something else.

Do not try to get other people to say things that are unkind or untrue.

Do not ask questions that will cause them to gossip.

Do not listen to people who want to gossip.
Do these things instead:

- Tell them kindly that you do not want to hear gossip.
- Go away from them if they continue gossiping.

You might feel hurt or angry when people gossip about you. You might want to gossip about them.

When people gossip about you, don't gossip about them. Do these things instead:

- Talk to them kindly. Ask them to stop gossiping about you.
- Try to work out your problems together. You may need to ask someone to help you.

You might feel like gossiping about people you do not know very well. Do not gossip about them. Do these things instead:

- Introduce yourself to the people.
- Get to know them and be kind to them.

It is important that you treat other people the way you want to be treated.

If you do not want people to gossip about you, you should not gossip about them.